ISBN 978-0-86163-871-0

First published 1999

Published by Award Publications Limited,
The Old Riding School, The Welbeck Estate,
Worksop, Nottinghamshire, S80 3LR

www.awardpublications.co.uk

5 7 9 10 8 6
08 10 12 14 16 18 20 19 17 15 13 11 09

Printed in Malaysia

Teddy's First Book of

PRAYERS

Illustrated by
Jane Launchbury

AWARD PUBLICATIONS
LIMITED

The Lord's Prayer

Our Father, who art in heaven,
Hallowed be thy name.
Thy kingdom come,
Thy will be done on earth
As it is in heaven.
Give us this day our daily bread
And forgive us our trespasses
As we forgive them
Who trespass against us.
And lead us not into temptation,
But deliver us from evil,
For thine is the kingdom,
The power and the glory,
For ever and ever

Amen.

If you have plenty, be not greedy,
But share it with the poor and needy:
If you have a little, take good care,
To give the little birds a share.

As I lay me down to sleep,
I pray thee, God, my soul to keep;
And in the morning, when I wake
Please make me good for Jesus' sake.

Thank you for the world so sweet,
Thank you for the things we eat,
Thank you for the birds that sing,
Thank you, God, for everything.

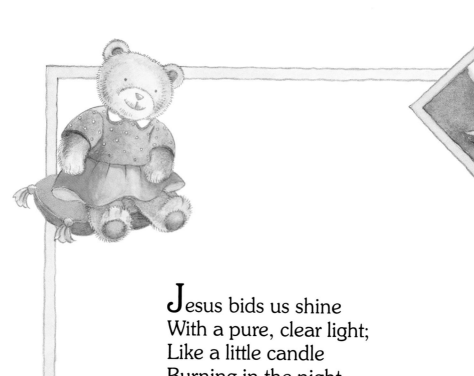

Jesus bids us shine
With a pure, clear light;
Like a little candle
Burning in the night.

In this world of darkness
We must shine;
You in your small corner
And I in mine.

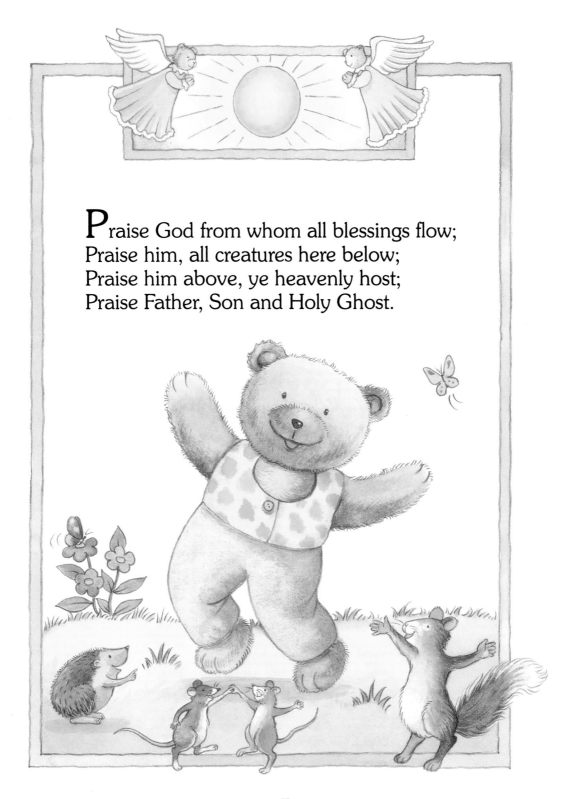

Praise God from whom all blessings flow;
Praise him, all creatures here below;
Praise him above, ye heavenly host;
Praise Father, Son and Holy Ghost.

Now the day is over,
Night is drawing nigh,
Shadows of the evening
Steal across the sky.

Now the darkness gathers,
Stars begin to peep,
Birds and beasts and flowers
Soon will be asleep.

Jesus give the weary
Calm and sweet repose;
With thy tenderest blessing
May our eyelids close.

Grant to little children
Visions bright of thee;
Guard the sailors tossing
On the deep blue sea.

When the morning wakens,
Then may I arise,
Pure, and fresh, and sinless
In thy holy eyes.

Thank you, God, for this new day
In my school to work and play.
Please be with me all day long,
In every story, game and song.
May all the happy things we do
Make you, our Father, happy too.

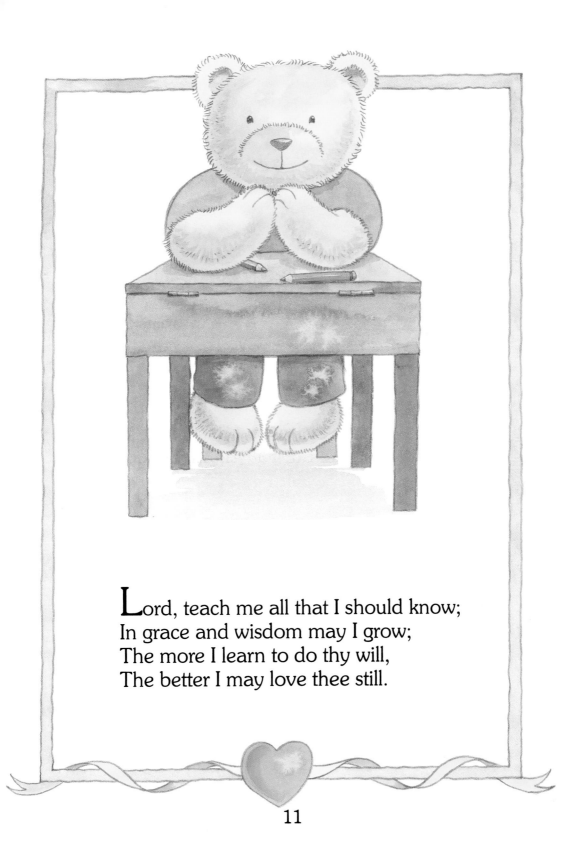

Lord, teach me all that I should know;
In grace and wisdom may I grow;
The more I learn to do thy will,
The better I may love thee still.

For flowers that bloom about our feet,
Father, we thank thee.
For the song of bird and hum of bee,
Father, we thank thee.
For all things fair we hear or see,
Father, we thank thee.

For blue of stream and blue of sky,
Father, we thank thee.
For pleasant shade of branches high,
Father, we thank thee.
For fragrant air and cooling breeze,
For the beauty of the blooming trees,
Father, we thank thee.

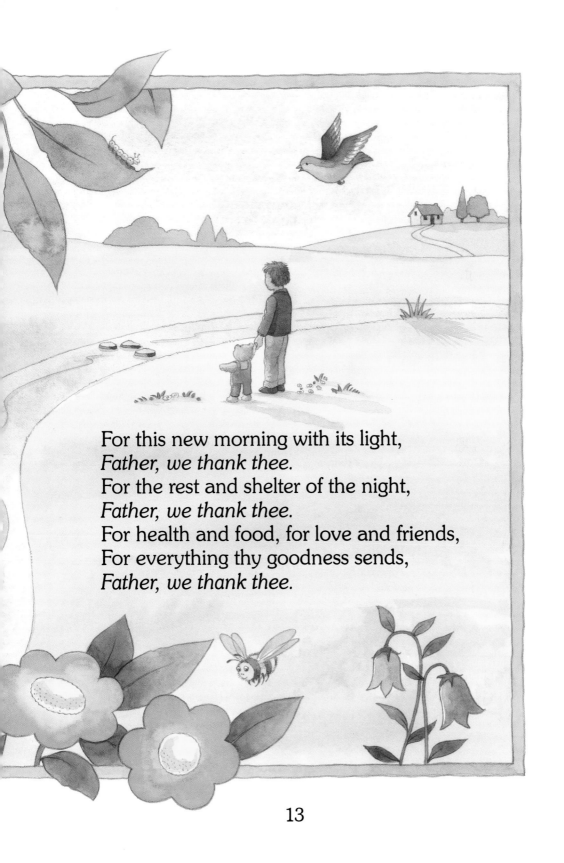

For this new morning with its light,
Father, we thank thee.
For the rest and shelter of the night,
Father, we thank thee.
For health and food, for love and friends,
For everything thy goodness sends,
Father, we thank thee.

Lord, make me an instrument of thy peace;
Where there is hatred, let me sow love;
Where there is injury, pardon;
Where there is discord, union;
Where there is doubt, faith;
Where there is despair, hope;
Where there is darkness, light;
Where there is sadness, joy.

Jesus, gentle shepherd, hear me,
Bless thy little lamb tonight.
Through the darkness be thou near me,
Watch my sleep till morning light.

All this day thy hand hath led me,
And I thank thee for thy care;
Thou hast clothed me, warmed and fed me;
Listen to my evening prayer.

May we in safety sleep tonight,
From every danger free;
Because the darkness and the light
Are both alike to thee.

And when the rising sun displays
His cheerful beams abroad,
Then shall our grateful voice of praise
Declare thy goodness, Lord.

What can I give him,
Poor as I am?
If I were a shepherd
I would bring him a lamb;
If I were a wise man
I would do my part;
Yet what I can I give him -
Give my heart.

Matthew, Mark, Luke and John
Bless the bed that I lie on.
Before I lay me down to sleep
I give my soul to Christ to keep.
Four corners to my bed,
Four angels overspread:
One at the head, one at the feet,
And two to guard me while I sleep.

I go by sea, I go by land,
The Lord made me with his right hand.
If any danger come to me,
Sweet Jesus Christ, deliver me.
He is the branch and I'm the flower,
May God send me a happy hour.

God bless the master of this house,
Likewise the mistress too,
And all the little children
That round the table go.

Father, lead me day by day,
Ever in thine own sweet way;
Teach me to be pure and true,
Show me what I ought to do.

When I'm tempted to do wrong,
Make me steadfast, wise and strong;
And when all alone I stand,
Shield me with thy mighty hand.

When my heart is full of glee,
Help me to remember thee;
Happy most of all to know
That my Father loves me so.

Bless these thy gifts, most gracious God
From whom all goodness springs,
Make clean our hearts and feed our souls
With good and joyful things.

Day by day, dear Lord of thee
Three things I pray:
To see thee more clearly,
To love thee more dearly,
To follow thee more nearly,
Day by day.

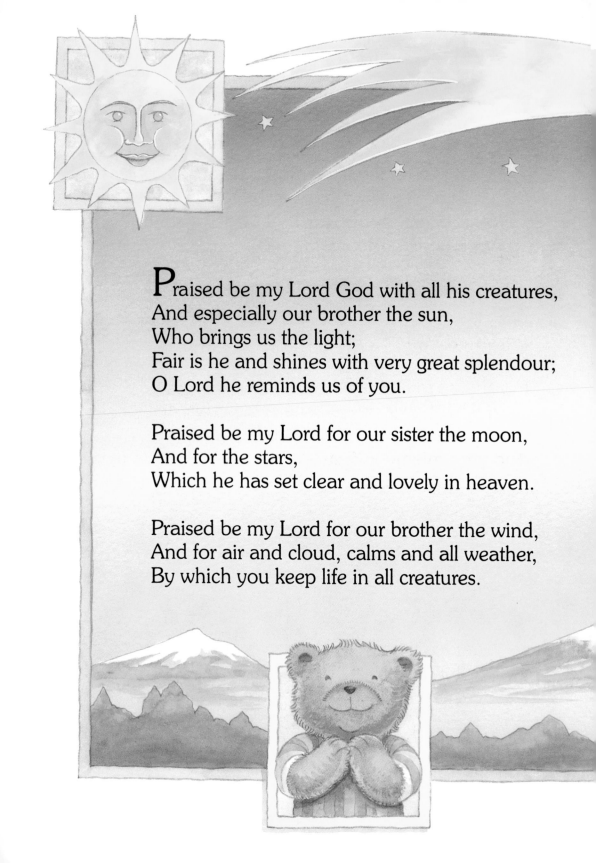

Praised be my Lord God with all his creatures,
And especially our brother the sun,
Who brings us the light;
Fair is he and shines with very great splendour;
O Lord he reminds us of you.

Praised be my Lord for our sister the moon,
And for the stars,
Which he has set clear and lovely in heaven.

Praised be my Lord for our brother the wind,
And for air and cloud, calms and all weather,
By which you keep life in all creatures.

Praised be my Lord for our sister water,
Who is very useful to us
And humble and precious and clean.

Praised be my Lord for our brother fire,
Through whom you gave us light in darkness;
And he is bright and pleasant
And very mighty and strong.

Praised be my Lord for our mother the earth,
Which feeds and keeps us,
And brings forth fruit,
And flowers of many colours, and grass.

Good Night! Good Night!
Far flies the light;
But still God's love
Shall flame above,
Making all bright.
Good Night! Good Night!

ACKNOWLEDGEMENTS
Many of the prayers in this book are traditional or by anonymous
writers. Where authors are known they are credited below.
Page 7: Bishop Ken; Page 8: S. Baring-Gould;
Page 11: Isaac Watts; Pages 12 & 13: Ralph Waldo Emerson;
Page 14: St. Francis of Assisi; Page 15: Mary L. Duncan;
Page 16: Jane Taylor; Page 17: Christina Rossetti;
Page 20: John Page Hopps;
Page 21 (bottom): St. Richard of Chichester;
Page 22 & 23: St. Francis of Assisi;
Page 24: Victor Hugo